The Uncrowned Queen

Appreciation Journal

By

Dr. Rev. Ahmondra McClendon

The Uncrowned Queen Appreciation Journal

Published by
Multi-faith Diversity Education
Carlsbad, CA

Copyright ©2022 by Dr. Rev. Ahmondra McClendon

Cover Design by Lionheart Creations
Interior Design by Dawn Teagarden

ISBN:
Hardback: 978-0-9859364-4-0
Paperback: 978-0-9859364-2-6

Printed in the United States of America

multifaithdiversityeducation.com

Cultivating Appreciation

Greetings, my Sistahs; I created this journal as a place for you to acknowledge and appreciate your magnificence. In this sacred space, you can express appreciation for your wisdom, the strength you've gained from past experiences, and the gift you are to the world. In addition, you can appreciate, honor, and recognize the ancestors for the sacrifices they made for us.

When we appreciate our beauty, we deepen our self-love and consciously engage with living. The word appreciate is a verb. When we appreciate something we are in action. And whatever we appreciate expands and increases.

As Black women from the African diaspora, we don't always acknowledge our brilliance. We are so busy nurturing others and safeguarding our community we forget about ourselves. We can become intertwined with another's dreams and desires and lose track of what is significant to us. Our dreams get put on the back burner indefinitely. Unfortunately, sometimes we forget they are even on the stove.

However, something miraculous happens when we recognize and appreciate who we are daily. We shift our focus, and we become the most important person in our lives. Our awareness of who we are expands. We start to remember those dreams sitting on the back burner and revisit them.

Demonstrating Appreciation

It is essential we create practices that keep the focus on us. It is so easy to get pulled away. A powerful way to demonstrate self-appreciation is to use rituals. Ritual is a sacred African practice that was lost to us. Through ritual, we, as African people, stayed connected to ourselves, each other, and the Divine. Rituals allowed us to pass down sacred practices, keeping them alive.

The I Appreciate Me (I A.M.) Ritual

The I A.M. Ritual is a simple yet powerful way to honor and show appreciation to ourselves. Daily practicing four simple steps can change your life.

Step 1
When you open your eyes each morning, consciously take a deep breath and say Thank You. You are expressing appreciation for being alive. Do not allow your thoughts to kidnap you into the daily tasks waiting to grab your attention. Do not make coffee, check your emails, or turn on the news because your mind will become preoccupied. Instead, keep your attention, and focus on yourself.

Step 2
You can leave the bedroom to sit in a quiet place or sit in bed. Always make sure your Appreciation Journal is close at hand. Close your eyes for a few moments, open them, and write down at least five things you appreciate about yourself. Ignore any thought that does not honor you or that diverts your focus. It can be challenging to ignore specific thoughts initially, but it will get easier.

Step 3

After making your entries, read something uplifting. It can be the message from a book of daily readings or a passage from a sacred text. The idea is to nourish your mind with empowering words.

Step 4

Close your eyes and end your ritual by speaking the words (out loud) I Appreciate Me today. (Put your journal back in the same place so it is available for the next day.) Then, begin your day with empowering thoughts about yourself.

Before performing the I A.M. ritual, you must refrain from conversing with anyone. You may have to train your household to wait until you complete your ritual before approaching you. Help them understand this is YOUR sacred time and needs to be honored.

You may also need to remind yourself how important this sacred time is. If an interruption surfaces, ask yourself, will delaying my response for five to ten minutes make a difference? Can it wait? You will usually find that it can. But if it cannot be delayed (because it is a life-or-death situation), ensure you find the time to complete the I A.M. ritual before the day is over. It is essential to carve out those five to ten minutes for yourself.

Sustaining Appreciation

Twenty-One Day Practice

The journal is designed with an entry for each day of the year. If you miss several days when you return to the journal, it will be evident how many days went by without ritual. In addition, you will quickly recognize how outside activities are taking precedence over you.

The practice will evolve into a habit if you practice the I A.M. ritual for twenty-one days straight (no breaks). This habit will become a solid foundation for building your day. It will also deepen your connection to the Divine and expand your appreciation for self. (If you miss a day before you reach twenty-one consecutive days, begin again. Do this until you accomplish practicing twenty-one days in a row. Don't get discouraged if you keep starting over. Instead, turn it into a personal challenge. Finally, one day you will complete a twenty-one day cycle.)

If you already have devotional time, please incorporate the steps of the I A.M. ritual into your sacred practice.

I invite you to introduce the I A.M. ritual to the young people in your life. Take them to a bookstore, where they can pick out a journal they like. Help them establish a sacred time to express self-appreciation. Helping them practice rituals will increase self-awareness, self-respect and develop discipline. Just imagine what your life might have looked like if you had learned to appreciate your uniqueness as a young person.

On A Personal Note

Before moving to Africa, I was not a fan of journal writing because I did not understand the benefits. For years I had tried to consistently practice journaling (even though I didn't think it was useful) because I heard how powerful it was. Even though I had half-filled journals all over the house, I never gave up trying.

While studying with Brother Ishmael Tetteh (ethereanlife.com), something shifted, and my attitude toward journaling changed. He re-introduced the practice as a powerful sacred ritual. I learned how daily journaling could strengthen my connection to myself and the Divine.

I made a commitment to daily journaling when I realized how this simple practice could expand self-awareness, deepen spiritual connection, and ignite enthusiasm for life. It wasn't just an exercise in futility; it allowed me to put focus on myself and appreciate who I was as a Divine Being.

After journaling for an entire year, I saw how acknowledging myself and appreciating my gifts had changed me. I had moved from putting others' concerns first to making myself the most important person in my life. I recognized the importance of sharing my gifts with the world in my unique way. What others believed about me was less important than what I believed about myself.

As you begin a new journal writing journey, I encourage you not to give up.

My sistahs, don't be discouraged if you start and stop or if it feels like an unrewarding task. You don't have to be perfect; you only need to strive for the goal of incorporating this sacred ritual into your daily life. Keep journaling until it becomes a habit.

Remember, consistency is the key.

You are worth appreciating, so make journaling a life-long practice.

Blessings,

Dr. Rev. Ahmondra McClendon

I Appreciate My

(Use this list on days you find it difficult to identify things to appreciate about yourself)

Strength	Warmth
Compassion	Diplomacy
Empathy	Organizational skills
Courage	Love of little children
Perseverance	Inner beautiful
Cooking skills	Body
Gift of gab	Party nature
Adventurous nature	Volunteerism
Comedic expression	Unique style
Devotion to God	Commitment to justice
Advocacy	Truth telling
Pride	Endurance level

I Appreciate my Ability & Willingness to

(Use this list on days you find it difficult to identify things to appreciate about yourself)

Nurture others

Sacrifice when I need to

Dance

Sing with my fantastic voice

Love my grandchildren

Be a great mother

Support others

Recognize others in need

Be a trailblazer

Be alone and thrive

To set boundaries

To set goals and reach them

To care for my physical body

Love my partner completely

Make personal change

Be an actress

Express my creativity

Support my friends

Walk to new paths

Change old patterns of behavior

Follow my intuition

Work hard and long

Express my feelings

Support my sistahs

Gye Nyame
God is all there is

" "

January

In Appreciation of Queen

_____
_____
_____

"Women must become revolutionary. This cannot be evolution but revolution."

~ Shirley Chisholm ~

JANUARY 1

_____
_____
_____
_____
_____

JANUARY 2

_____
_____
_____
_____
_____

JANUARY 3

_____
_____
_____
_____
_____

JANUARY 4

JANUARY 5

JANUARY 6

JANUARY 7

JANUARY 8

JANUARY 9

JANUARY 10

JANUARY 11

*"Do not desire to fit in.
Desire to oblige yourselves to lead."*

~ Gwendolyn Brooks~

JANUARY 12

_____
_____
_____
_____

JANUARY 13

_____
_____
_____
_____

JANUARY 14

_____
_____
_____
_____

JANUARY 15

JANUARY 16

JANUARY 17

"Power is not given to you. You have to take it."
~ Beyoncé Knowles ~

JANUARY 18

JANUARY 19

JANUARY 20

JANUARY 21

JANUARY 22

JANUARY 23

JANUARY 24

JANUARY 25

"We must always attempt to lift as we climb."
~Angela Davis~

JANUARY 26

_____
_____
_____
_____
_____

JANUARY 27

_____
_____
_____
_____
_____

JANUARY 28

_____
_____
_____
_____
_____

JANUARY 29

JANUARY 30

JANUARY 31

"When you are willing to make sacrifices for a great cause, you will never be alone."

~ Coretta Scott King~

February

In Appreciation of Queen

_____
_____
_____

"Success is liking yourself, liking what you do, and liking how you do it."

~ Maya Angelou ~

FEBRUARY 1

FEBRUARY 2

FEBRUARY 3

FEBRUARY 4

FEBRUARY 5

FEBRUARY 6

FEBRUARY 7

FEBRUARY 8

FEBRUARY 9

FEBRUARY 10

FEBRUARY 11

"If we give our children sound self-love, they will be able to deal with whatever life puts before them."

~ Bell Hooks ~

FEBRUARY 12

_____
_____
_____
_____
_____

FEBRUARY 13

_____
_____
_____
_____
_____

FEBRUARY 14

_____
_____
_____
_____
_____

FEBRUARY 15

FEBRUARY 16

FEBRUARY 17

"You've got to learn to leave the table when love's no longer being served."

~ Nina Simone ~

FEBRUARY 18

FEBRUARY 19

FEBRUARY 20

FEBRUARY 21

FEBRUARY 22

FEBRUARY 23

FEBRUARY 24

FEBRUARY 25

"Even if it makes others uncomfortable,"
"I will love who I am."
~Janelle Monáe~

FEBRUARY 26

___
___
___
___

FEBRUARY 27

___
___
___
___

FEBRUARY 28

___
___
___
___

FEBRUARY 29

_____
_____
_____
_____
_____

"Caring for myself is not self-indulgence, it is self-preservation, and that is an act of political warfare."

~Audre Lorde~

March

In Appreciation of Queen

_____

_____

_____

"Breathe. Let go. And remind yourself that this very moment is the only one you know you have for sure."

~Oprah Winfrey~

MARCH 1

_____
_____
_____
_____
_____

MARCH 2

_____
_____
_____
_____
_____

MARCH 3

_____
_____
_____
_____
_____

MARCH 4

MARCH 5

MARCH 6

MARCH 7

MARCH 8

MARCH 9

MARCH 10

MARCH 11

"You can fall, but you can rise also."
~Angelique Kidjo~

MARCH 12

_____
_____
_____
_____
_____

MARCH 13

_____
_____
_____
_____
_____

MARCH 14

_____
_____
_____
_____
_____

MARCH 15

MARCH 16

MARCH 17

"Life is short, and it's up to you to make it sweet."
~ Sadie Delany ~

MARCH 18

MARCH 19

MARCH 20

MARCH 21

MARCH 22

MARCH 23

MARCH 24

MARCH 25

"Don't settle for average. Bring your best to the moment. Then, whether it fails or succeeds, at least you know you gave all you had. We need to live the best that's in us."

~Angela Bassett~

MARCH 26

_____
_____
_____
_____

MARCH 27

_____
_____
_____
_____

MARCH 28

_____
_____
_____
_____

MARCH 29

MARCH 30

MARCH 31

"If you prioritize yourself, you are going to save yourself."
~ Gabrielle Union ~

April

In Appreciation of Queen

_____
_____
_____

*"Don't wait around for other people to be happy for you.
Any Happiness you get you've got to make yourself."*

~Alice Walker~

APRIL 1

APRIL 2

APRIL 3

APRIL 4

APRIL 5

APRIL 6

APRIL 7

APRIL 8

APRIL 9

APRIL 10

APRIL 11

"You will be wounded many times in your life. You'll make mistakes. Some people will call them failures, but I have learned that failure is really God's way of saying, Excuse me, you're moving in the wrong direction. It's just an experience, just an experience."

~Oprah Winfrey~

APRIL 12

APRIL 13

APRIL 14

APRIL 15

APRIL 16

APRIL 17

"You've just got to follow your own path. You have to trust your heart and you have to listen to the warnings."

~ Chaka Khan ~

APRIL 18

APRIL 19

APRIL 20

APRIL 21

APRIL 22

APRIL 23

APRIL 24

APRIL 25

"Deal with yourself as an individual worthy of respect, and make everyone else deal with you the same way."

~ Nikki Giovanni ~

APRIL 26

APRIL 27

APRIL 28

APRIL 29

_____
_____
_____
_____
_____

APRIL 30

_____
_____
_____
_____
_____

"When you put love out in the world it travels, and it can touch people and reach people in ways that we never even expected."

~Laverne Cox~

May

In Appreciation of Queen

_____
_____
_____

"I have learned over the years that when one's mind is made up, this diminishes fear; knowing what must be done does away with fear."

~ Rosa Parks ~

MAY 1

___

MAY 2

___

MAY 3

___

MAY 4

MAY 5

MAY 6

MAY 7

MAY 8

MAY 9

MAY 10

MAY 11

MAY 12

MAY 13

MAY 14

MAY 15

MAY 16

MAY 17

MAY 18

MAY 19

MAY 20

MAY 21

MAY 22

MAY 23

MAY 24

MAY 25

MAY 26

MAY 27

MAY 28

MAY 29

MAY 30

MAY 31

June

In Appreciation of

Queen

_____

_____

> *"I thrive on obstacles. If I'm told that it can't be told, then I push harder."*
>
> *~Issa Rae~*

JUNE 1

JUNE 2

JUNE 3

JUNE 4

JUNE 5

JUNE 6

JUNE 7

JUNE 8

JUNE 9

JUNE 10

JUNE 11

"I don't have to go around trying to save everybody anymore; that's not my job."

~ Jada Pinkett Smith ~

JUNE 12

JUNE 13

JUNE 14

JUNE 15

JUNE 16

JUNE 17

> *"One of the lessons that I grew up with was to always stay true to yourself and never let what somebody else says distract you from your goals."*
>
> ~ *Michelle Obama* ~

JUNE 18

JUNE 19

JUNE 20

JUNE 21

JUNE 22

JUNE 23

JUNE 24

JUNE 25

"My mission in life is not merely to survive but to thrive; and to do so with some passion, some compassion, some humor, and some style."

~ Maya Angelou ~

JUNE 26

_____
_____
_____
_____
_____

JUNE 27

_____
_____
_____
_____
_____

JUNE 28

_____
_____
_____
_____
_____

JUNE 29

JUNE 30

"You may not always have a comfortable life and you will not always be able to solve all of the world's problems at once but don't ever underestimate the importance you can have because history has shown us that courage can be contagious, and hope can take on a life of its own."

~ Michelle Obama ~

July

In Appreciation of Queen

_____

_____

_____

"Be passionate and move forward with gusto every single hour of every single day until you reach your goal."

~Ava DuVernay~

JULY 1

JULY 2

JULY 3

JULY 4

JULY 5

JULY 6

JULY 7

JULY 8

JULY 9

JULY 10

JULY 11

"It was when I realized I needed to stop trying to be somebody else and be myself, I actually started to own, accept and love what I had."

~ Tracee Ellis Ross ~

JULY 12

_____
_____
_____
_____

JULY 13

_____
_____
_____
_____

JULY 14

_____
_____
_____
_____

JULY 15

JULY 16

JULY 17

"Freeing yourself was one thing; claiming ownership of that freed self was another."

~ Toni Morrison ~

JULY 18

JULY 19

JULY 20

JULY 21

JULY 22

JULY 23

JULY 24

JULY 25

"The first sign of an educated person is that she asks more questions than she delivers."

~Johnnetta B. Coles~

JULY 26

JULY 27

JULY 28

JULY 29

_____
_____
_____
_____
_____

JULY 30

_____
_____
_____
_____
_____

JULY 31

_____
_____
_____
_____
_____

"You deserve safety. You deserve protection.
You deserve love. You deserve peace."

~Tarana Burke~

August

In Appreciation of Queen

_____

_____

"I will not have my life narrowed down. I will not bow down to somebody else's whim or to someone else's ignorance."

~Bell Hooks~

AUGUST 1

AUGUST 2

AUGUST 3

AUGUST 4

AUGUST 5

AUGUST 6

AUGUST 7

AUGUST 8

AUGUST 9

AUGUST 10

AUGUST 11

"Give light and people will find the way."
~Ella Baker~

AUGUST 12

AUGUST 13

AUGUST 14

AUGUST 15

AUGUST 16

AUGUST 17

"Whatever is bringing you down, get rid of it. Because you'll find that when you're free...your true self comes out."

~ Tina Turner ~

AUGUST 18

AUGUST 19

AUGUST 20

AUGUST 21

AUGUST 22

AUGUST 23

AUGUST 24

AUGUST 25

> *"I'm convinced that we Black women possess a special indestructible strength that allows us to not only get down, but to get up, to get through, and to get over."*
> ~Janet Jackson~

AUGUST 26

_____
_____
_____
_____
_____

AUGUST 27

_____
_____
_____
_____
_____

AUGUST 28

_____
_____
_____
_____
_____

AUGUST 29

_____
_____
_____
_____

AUGUST 30

_____
_____
_____
_____

AUGUST 31

_____
_____
_____
_____

"Surround yourself with only people who are going to lift you higher."
~ Oprah Winfrey ~

September

In Appreciation of

_____
_____
_____

"There's always something to suggest that you'll never be who you wanted to be. Your choice is to take it or keep on moving."

~ Phylicia Rashad ~

SEPTEMBER 1

_____
_____
_____
_____
_____

SEPTEMBER 2

_____
_____
_____
_____
_____

SEPTEMBER 3

_____
_____
_____
_____
_____

SEPTEMBER 4

SEPTEMBER 5

SEPTEMBER 6

SEPTEMBER 7

SEPTEMBER 8

SEPTEMBER 9

SEPTEMBER 10

SEPTEMBER 11

"Wisdom is higher than a fool can reach."
~ Phillis Wheatley ~

SEPTEMBER 12

SEPTEMBER 13

SEPTEMBER 14

SEPTEMBER 15

SEPTEMBER 16

SEPTEMBER 17

"I think there are things for all of us to do as long as we're here and we're healthy."

~ Gwendolyn Brooks ~

SEPTEMBER 18

SEPTEMBER 19

SEPTEMBER 20

SEPTEMBER 21

SEPTEMBER 22

SEPTEMBER 23

SEPTEMBER 24

SEPTEMBER 25

"Once we recognize what it is we are feeling, once we recognize we can feel deeply, love deeply, can feel joy, then we will demand that all parts of our lives produce that kind of joy."

~ Audre Lorde ~

SEPTEMBER 26

SEPTEMBER 27

SEPTEMBER 28

SEPTEMBER 29

SEPTEMBER 30

> "Trust yourself. Think for yourself. Act for yourself. Speak for yourself. Be yourself. Imitation is suicide."
>
> ~ Marva Collins ~

October

In Appreciation of Queen

_____
_____

"I have standards I don't plan on lowering for anybody...including myself."

~ Zendaya ~

OCTOBER 1

OCTOBER 2

OCTOBER 3

OCTOBER 4

OCTOBER 5

OCTOBER 6

OCTOBER 7

OCTOBER 8

OCTOBER 9

OCTOBER 10

OCTOBER 11

OCTOBER 12

OCTOBER 13

OCTOBER 14

OCTOBER 15

OCTOBER 16

_____
_____
_____
_____
_____

OCTOBER 17

_____
_____
_____
_____
_____

"I always believed that when you follow your heart or your gut, when you really follow the things that feel great to you, you can never lose, because settling is the worst feeling in the world."

~Rihanna~

OCTOBER 18

OCTOBER 19

OCTOBER 20

OCTOBER 21

OCTOBER 22

OCTOBER 23

OCTOBER 24

OCTOBER 25

"African women, in general, need to know that it's OK for them to be the way they are – to see the way they are as a strength, and to be liberated from fear and from silence."

~ Wangari Maathai ~

OCTOBER 26

OCTOBER 27

OCTOBER 28

OCTOBER 29

OCTOBER 30

OCTOBER 31

"In every crisis there is a message. Crises are nature's way of forcing change – breaking down old structures, shaking loose negative habits so that something new and better can take their place."

~Susan L. Taylor~

November

In Appreciation of

Queen

> *"There's so many things that life is, and no matter how many breakthroughs, trials will exist and we're going to get through it. Just be strong."*
>
> ~ Mary J. Blige ~

NOVEMBER 1

_____
_____
_____
_____
_____

NOVEMBER 2

_____
_____
_____
_____
_____

NOVEMBER 3

_____
_____
_____
_____
_____

NOVEMBER 4

NOVEMBER 5

NOVEMBER 6

NOVEMBER 7

NOVEMBER 8

NOVEMBER 9

NOVEMBER 10

NOVEMBER 11

"Success doesn't come to you...you go to it."
~ Marva Collins ~

NOVEMBER 12

_____
_____
_____
_____
_____

NOVEMBER 13

_____
_____
_____
_____
_____

NOVEMBER 14

_____
_____
_____
_____
_____

NOVEMBER 15

NOVEMBER 16

NOVEMBER 17

*"I'd rather regret the risks that didn't work out
than the chances I didn't take at all."*

~ Simone Biles ~

NOVEMBER 18

NOVEMBER 19

NOVEMBER 20

NOVEMBER 21

NOVEMBER 22

NOVEMBER 23

NOVEMBER 24

NOVEMBER 25

"Never limit yourself because of others' limited imagination; never limit others because of your own limited imagination."

~ Dr. Mae Jemison ~

NOVEMBER 26

NOVEMBER 27

NOVEMBER 28

NOVEMBER 29

NOVEMBER 30

"The kind of beauty I want most is the hard-to-get kind that comes from within – strength, courage, dignity."

~ Ruby Dee ~

December

In Appreciation of

_____
_____

I did my best, and God did the rest."
~Hattie McDaniel~

DECEMBER 1

DECEMBER 2

DECEMBER 3

DECEMBER 4

DECEMBER 5

DECEMBER 6

DECEMBER 7

DECEMBER 8

DECEMBER 9

DECEMBER 10

DECEMBER 11

"There is always light. If only we're brave enough to see it. If only we're brave enough to be it."

~Amanda Gorman~

DECEMBER 12

_____
_____
_____
_____
_____

DECEMBER 13

_____
_____
_____
_____
_____

DECEMBER 14

_____
_____
_____
_____
_____

DECEMBER 15

DECEMBER 16

DECEMBER 17

"I didn't learn to be quiet when I had an opinion. The reason they knew who I was is because I told them."

~ Ursula Burns ~

DECEMBER 18

DECEMBER 19

DECEMBER 20

DECEMBER 21

DECEMBER 22

DECEMBER 23

DECEMBER 24

DECEMBER 25

"Black women can do anything. We have proven that time and time and time again."

~ Tarana Burke ~

DECEMBER 26

DECEMBER 27

DECEMBER 28

DECEMBER 29

DECEMBER 30

DECEMBER 31

"Don't ever let anyone make you feel like you don't matter. Or like you don't have a place in our American story; because you do. And you have a right to be exactly who you are."

~ Michelle Obama ~

Queens

I honored this year were

My Intentions

For the upcoming year

_____

About Dr. Rev. Ahmondra McClendon

Rev. Ahmondra is an Interfaith Minister, Progressive Christian Minister, Trainer, Inspirational Speaker, Published Author, Spiritual Mentor/Advisor, and Certified Master Facilitator. She holds a Master of Social Work Degree from San Francisco State University and a Doctor of Ministry Degree from New York Theological Seminary.

Although her life is in harmony today, it wasn't always. For decades Rev. Ahmondra existed behind a wall of silence in a world filled with painful secrets. Yet, all the while, she acted as if everything was all right.

Realizing that circumstances did not have to determine her future, she broke the silence and spoke her truth. With each secret exposed, a new possibility opened to her. She moved from victimhood to victory with sistahs' support and unconditional love.

Understanding that Black women flourish when together Rev. Ahmondra created The Original Queens Sacred Community. In this safe space, sistahs gather to learn, grow, share, heal, and empower each other along life's journey.

You are invited to join Rev. Ahmondra and other Sistahs as they rewrite new narratives, reclaim their identity as original queens, and create lives unburdened by past trauma.

Register at:
Originalqueens.net

or

Contact Rev. Ahmondra directly at:
revahmondra@originalqueens.net

www.ingramcontent.com/pod-product-compliance
Lightning Source LLC
Chambersburg PA
CBHW062115290426
44110CB00028B/2770